St. Monica Ministry Manual

A guide for
drawing your loved ones
back to the Church

Celeste Behe

En Route Books and Media, LLC
Saint Louis, MO

⊕ENROUTE
Make the time

En Route Books and Media, LLC
5705 Rhodes Avenue
St. Louis, MO 63109

Contact us at
contactus@enroutebooksandmedia.com

Cover Credit: Celeste Behe
Copyright 2025 Celeste Behe

ISBN-13: 979-8-88870-451-6
Library of Congress Control Number:
Available online at https://catalog.loc.gov

Nihil Obstat: Deacon Christopher May
Censor Librorum

Imprimatur: Most Reverend Alfred A. Schlert
Bishop of Allentown

The *Nihil Obstat* and the *Imprimatur* are a declaration that a book or pamphlet is considered to be free from doctrinal or moral error. It is not implied that those who have granted the *Nihil Obstat* or *Imprimatur* agree with the contents, opinions, or statements expressed therein.

All rights reserved. No part of this book may be reproduced, stored in a retrieval system, or transmitted in any form, or by any means, electronic, mechanical, photocopying, or otherwise, without the prior written permission of the author.

Table of Contents

Foreword by Bishop Alfred A. Schlert iii

About the St. Monica Ministry™ 1

Building Community 2

Laying the Groundwork 3

Supplying Your Meeting Space 7

The "stuff" you need 7

What Does a Meeting Look Like? 11

The St. Monica Ministry™ Holy Hour of Petition and Hope 17

    Basic Supplies 18

    Candles of Entreaty 18

    The Book of Petition and Hope 19

    Icon of St. Monica 20

The St. Monica Ministry "Rosary of Supplication for Our Prodigals":
Meditations for Each of the Twenty Mysteries of the Rosary 23

The "Wayfaring St. Monica" Program 31

Prayer of the St. Monica Ministry to its Patron 34

St. Monica Ministry Sample Meeting Agenda 35

Recommended Reading 36

Foreword

I hear the laments over and over as I travel around the Diocese.

"When I was growing up, we used to go together as a family to Mass, but my siblings have all left the Church."

"Our children were raised in the Faith, but since going out into the world, it seems their faith has evaporated. What did we do wrong?"

"My parents were daily communicants, but now, since COVID, they no longer go to Mass, even on Sunday."

Many, if not most, faithful Catholics have loved ones who are not involved in the sacramental life of the Church. Supporting those Catholics with both prayer and compassion is the St. Monica Ministry, a vibrant and much-needed outreach that we are very blessed to have in the Diocese of Allentown. Other dioceses have come to see what the ministry does and how it works, and they are eager to bring the St. Monica Ministry into their own parishes. Created to meet those demands, the *St. Monica Ministry Manual* not only enables dioceses to implement the St. Monica Ministry program, but it also equips the average Catholic in the pew to establish a parish-based St. Monica Ministry chapter.

Serving as the inspiration and intercessor for the ministry is St. Monica, who was herself the mother of a prodigal. Her son

Augustine, a brilliant but wayward young man, led a dissolute life that caused his mother untold pain. For many years, Monica prayed unrelentingly for her son, and not only did Augustine ultimately become a Christian, he became a Saint and a Doctor of the Church.

If we look closely at Monica's life, nowhere do we see that she nagged Augustine. I'm sure that Monica had some frank conversations with her son. I'm sure she expressed her displeasure at the life he was leading in the world, but she focused instead on prayer. She chose to "nag" God, and that is what He wants: for us to come incessantly to Him in prayer. In the end, it is an action of the Holy Spirit that brings someone back. We turn our prodigal over to God because, before that person was your son or sister, or daughter or spouse, he or she was a child of God.

It is significant that the Gospel reading for the August 27 Memorial of St. Monica is the account of the widow of Naim. This poor widow had no one left in the world but her son, and when her son died, she was grief-stricken. Jesus saw the widow's grief, and He responded by bringing her son back to life.

The widow's son was physically dead. Monica's son Augustine was spiritually dead. In both cases, Jesus perceived the situation and responded out of compassion, restoring life to the lifeless.

Prayer can bring back our loved ones who have strayed from the life of the Church. The program outlined in the *St. Monica Ministry Manual for Parishes* is founded on this conviction. The components of the program - the St. Monica Ministry Holy Hour, the Rosary of Supplication for Our Prodigals, the Candles of Entreaty, the Book of Petition and Hope, and even the meetings and book discussions – are guided by, and firmly rooted in, prayer.

I myself have had the occasion to preside at a St. Monica Ministry Holy Hour, and I have prayed the Rosary of Supplication together with those who are seeking their loved ones' return to the Church. I have witnessed firsthand the efficacy and beauty of shared petition. And I can attest that our constant prayer means a great deal before the throne of God.

No one is beyond God's grace, and nowhere is that truth more clearly exemplified than in the life of St. Augustine. Augustine himself, in his *Confessions*, wrote that his prayerful mother gave birth to him twice: once in the flesh, and again, in the spirit. Our prayer is that we might see the second birth of our loved ones, their birth in the Spirit.

The *St. Monica Ministry Manual for Parishes* can help bring about that yearned-for rebirth by inspiring dioceses, parishes, and individuals to pray as St. Monica did: humbly, resolutely, and with confidence. We know that is the surest road to salvation for our fallen-away loved ones, and we know that it is the surest road to our own salvation as well.

+Bishop Alfred A. Schlert
Diocese of Allentown, PA

About the St. Monica Ministry™

The St. Monica Ministry™ is both a dedicated community and prayer network offering hope and support to the families and friends of fallen-away Catholics. Like St. Monica, its members pray, fast, and care unconditionally for loved ones who have left the Church. Animated by hope and grounded in faith, we rest secure in the knowledge that, in the words of St. Monica, "Nothing is far from God."

The St. Monica Ministry™ was formed in November 2022 at the behest of the Most Reverend Alfred A. Schlert, Bishop of Allentown. Due to both the distinctive spirituality of the St. Monica Ministry™ and its nature as an official initiative of the Diocese of Allentown, it is important that uniformity be maintained in the practices and activities of St. Monica Ministry™ chapters within and without the diocese. By following the guidelines set forth in this manual, parish-based chapters of the St. Monica Ministry™ will help to maintain the necessary uniformity.

Building Community

As of July, 2025, thirty-two chapters of the St. Monica Ministry have been established in the U.S. In order to help us meet the needs of those who would benefit from the sense of community provided by the St. Monica Ministry™, we ask that you notify the ministry of nascent chapters. Contact information on those chapters will be listed on the St. Monica Ministry™ web page and in its newsletter, so that individuals may either connect with St. Monica Ministry™ communities in their area, or choose to form chapters in their own parishes.

Please note that the St. Monica Ministry's official icon of St. Monica (see book cover) is being trademarked, and that the contents of this manual are copyrighted. Before using any of these materials in your parish, please email StMonicaMinistry27@gmail.com to register your St. Monica Ministry chapter. There are no fees associated with registration, although donations are always gratefully accepted. Donations may be mailed c/o Celeste Behe, 2258 Apple Street, Bethlehem, PA 18015. While chapters are asked to conform to the guidelines in this manual, their members are warmly invited to offer suggestions for program improvements.

The St. Monica Ministry humbly requests your prayers for the furtherance of its work, according to God's will.

Questions, comments, and stories of reversion may be sent to the above email address.

Laying the Groundwork

Begin As We Begin All Things

Start with prayer.

And Then

Obtain your pastor's permission for your group to meet on parish grounds. Although Father is likely to be supportive of a prayer-focused venture like the St. Monica Ministry™, there may be administrative considerations preventing him from giving his approval right away. Be patient.

Once you have the pastor's go-ahead, secure a meeting place. Don't count on the ready availability of the pleasant little meeting room that you've been eyeing. Remember that the space demands of parish groups tend to change with both the climatic and liturgical seasons, so the meeting space that today appears to be a forgotten gem may one month from now be in near-constant use. Avoid disappointment by following the parish protocol for reserving the room that you think will best suit your group's needs. When making your request, be ready with a list of meeting dates so that you can, if your parish allows, reserve a year's worth of meeting space in one fell swoop.

About Those Meeting Dates and Times

The demographics of your parish will have some bearing on the scheduling of St. Monica Ministry™ chapter meetings. Are there grandparents who are interested in joining, but who may have trouble traveling after dark? Daytime meetings would be the most practical option for them. Are there many parents of fallen-away college students who would benefit from the emotional support provided by the ministry? Evening meetings would be more likely to suit their work schedules. Here at the St. Monica Ministry™ home parish, we hold two meetings per month, both of which follow the same meeting agenda. In order to accommodate different schedules, one of the two meetings takes place during morning hours and the other in the evening. While daytime meetings are better attended, the evening meetings are the ones that tend to draw couples. This may or may not be the case in your parish. Pray for guidance before you take the scheduling plunge. And remember that nothing you do is "set in stone."

A period of trial and error is very likely to accompany the early days of your St. Monica Ministry™ group. *Don't ever hesitate to contact the ministry for help with any kind of issue.*

Regarding meeting frequency, either once or twice a month should be sufficient, though weekly meetings can work as long as there's interest. If your group is particularly enthused, you might plan an "extra" gathering after the monthly Holy Hour (see page 17), for the express purpose of enjoying some fellowship.

"Pray for Our Prodigals"

Not everyone with fallen-away loved ones is either able or inclined to attend meetings or Holy Hours. For those individuals, as well as for other members of the parish, it is good to offer a place where intentions may be submitted at one's own convenience, with the assurance that the intentions will be lifted up in prayer. A "Pray for Our Prodigals" intentions box allows the members of a St. Monica Ministry™ community to pray for prodigals who are outside of their own family and friend circles. Any box may be used for this purpose, as long as its contents may be kept secure. The box may be attractive on its own, e.g., a decorative hatbox, or it may be a grocery store box that has been covered in kraft paper or giftwrap. In the top panel of the box, cut out a slot just wide enough to accommodate the slips that will be deposited in the box. Adhesive letters, hand-lettering, or an ordinary printer-paper printout should clearly designate the box as the "Pray for Our Prodigals" intentions box. *Be sure to include the words "Sponsored by the [name of your parish] St. Monica Ministry."* In order to increase the visibility of the box, as well as to help form an association with other events sponsored by your group - such as the monthly Holy Hours and the "Wayfaring St. Monica" program – there should be an image of the official icon (see page 20) placed on or near the "Pray for Our Prodigals" box. Also nearby should be a box, basket, or other receptacle containing blank slips of paper on which prayer requestors may write the names of their prodigals before depositing the slips in the box. For requestors' convenience, have plenty of pencils or pens at hand. (Pencils are less expensive and neater than pens, and they work well for our purpose.) The box, image, slips, and pens/pencils should be placed either at the back of the church or in the church vestibule, with your pastor's permission. Slips will be collected prior to St. Monica Ministry™ meetings (see page 14). It is recommended that the "Pray for Our Prodigals" intentions box be introduced via an announcement made after weekend Masses.

Supplying Your Meeting Space
The "stuff" you need

Sign-In Sheet

Your sign-in sheet can be a spiral-bound notebook page, a legal pad, a leaf in a composition book, or anything else on which attendance can be noted. Upon arrival at the meeting, each participant is invited to add his name, email address, cell phone number, and name of parish to the sign-in sheet. The information provided will enable the facilitator to follow up with first-time attendees, notify participants of last-minute changes to meeting schedules, and the like.

Meeting Agendas

Printed agendas provide participants with clear meeting objectives and time frames, while also letting them know what to expect from a meeting. (A sample meeting agenda can be found on page 35.) Agendas should be placed beside the sign-in sheet for participants to pick up as they enter the meeting room. More about meeting agendas can be found on page 11 under the heading, **What Does a Meeting Look Like?**

Name Tags

As a support community, the St. Monica Ministry™ has a strongly relational dimension. It speaks to those who (1) need to talk about their experiences, (2) may feel isolated in their faith community as a result of their prodigals' rejection of the Faith, (3) find that others don't understand what they are going through, and (4) would benefit from listening to others share their stories. In order to provide the needed support, the St. Monica Ministry™ values every participant, not only as a member of the ministry, but as a unique child of God. For that reason, we follow St. John the Evangelist's instruction to "Greet the friends there, each by name," by inviting each meeting participant to wear a name tag. Name tags and markers should be placed near the agendas, to be filled out upon participants' arrival.

Palliatives

According to participants, one of the most valued aspects of the St. Monica Ministry™ is its offering of a "space" in which participants are free to express their grief over a loved one's loss of faith. Emotions at meetings can run high, so be prepared with tissues, bottled water, and the like.

Prayer of the St. Monica Ministry™ to its Patron

The official Prayer of the St. Monica Ministry™ to its Patron, recited at the start of each meeting, may be found on page 34 of this manual. The prayer may be printed for distribution to meeting participants, or simply added to the meeting agenda for convenience (and to practice good stewardship by saving on paper).

Alternatively, chapters may request prayer cards imprinted with the Prayer of the St. Monica Ministry™. Please send requests to StMonicaMinistry27@gmail.com. **When requesting prayer cards, please specify your choice of English or Spanish language.** There is no charge for the cards, but donations are accepted.

Rosaries

Since the praying of the rosary is at the heart of each St. Monica Ministry™ meeting, there should be rosaries available for use by attendees who may not have brought rosaries with them. Also, consider putting out "How to Pray the Rosary" pamphlets for the benefit of those who may not be accustomed to praying the rosary. (Marian Press offers an inexpensive pamphlet at **shopmercy.org/pray-the-rosary-daily.html**) More on rosary recitation will be found on page 13 in the **What Does a Meeting Look Like?** section of this manual.

What Does a Meeting Look Like?

Meetings run for 90 minutes. In order to respect the schedules of those attending, meetings should start and end on time. Printed agendas containing time allotments can help to keep meetings on track.

A St. Monica Ministry™ meeting has seven components:

- Opening Prayer

- Announcements

- Welcome / Introductions

- Shares

- Rosary

- Book discussion

- "Pray for Our Prodigals" intercessions

- Closing Prayer

Opening Prayer

Each meeting opens with group recitation of the "Prayer of the St. Monica Ministry™ to its Patron," the text of which may be supplied to participants as either a handout or a printed prayer card (see pages 8-9.) The "Prayer of the St. Monica Ministry™ to its Patron" may be found on page 34 of this manual.

Announcements

The facilitator may make announcements that are relevant to the group's purpose. A change in the meeting schedule, a timely podcast recommendation, details of the group's next Holy Hour: Any of these may be mentioned during the Announcements segment.

Welcome / Introductions

During this segment, the facilitator invites each participant to identify himself and briefly share his reason for attending the meeting.

Shares

Since the inception of the St. Monica Ministry™ in November, 2022, many people with prodigal loved ones have unburdened themselves in emails to the ministry. "I feel responsible for my kids leaving the Church…" "I have been praying for many years, but my daughter still doesn't go to Mass…" There is much hurt, but there is also hope: "Being with other people who are going through the same thing is incredibly helpful…" "I've been praying for a group like this…" "Now I know I'm not the only one…" Because God made us for relationship, the Shares segment of the meeting is especially important. During this segment, participants are welcome to report on recent developments in their prodigals' journey back to the faith. They may also make prayer requests or recommend resources that they have found helpful.

Rosary

Recited within the framework of a meeting, the rosary renews the group's sense of purpose and unifies participants in hope. It is recommended that, in order to keep the meeting on schedule, the optional prayers of the rosary be omitted. Note that the Rosary of Supplication for Prodigals (see page 23), with its meditations, is normally recited only during Holy Hours and as part of the Wayfaring St. Monica program.

Book Discussion

As a book to "kick off" discussion at a newly-formed St. Monica Ministry™ chapter, Brandon Vogt's *Return: How to Draw Your Child Back to the Church* is highly recommended. Although the book is directed at parents, its "game plan" to draw Catholics back to the Church is a boon to anyone who loves a prodigal. Bonus: A free downloadable book discussion guide can be found at www.wordonfire.org/return/

A list of additional titles for book discussion may be found on page 36 of this manual.

The facilitator is responsible for keeping book discussions on topic and for maintaining a positive group dynamic, both inside and outside of the discussion segment of the meeting. There is no special skill or training needed to fulfill this role; all that is required is that the facilitator lead with love, bearing in mind each participant's worth in Christ.

"Pray for Our Prodigals" intercessions

During this segment of the meeting, all present pray for those whose names have been written on the "Pray for Our Prodigals" slips (see page 5). The slips would have been collected from the "Pray for Our Prodigals" box just before the start of the meeting, and then distributed among the meeting participants. A simple introductory prayer may be offered by a member of the group, e.g. "Lord, through the intercession of St. Monica, we pray for these your children who have fallen away from the Faith." Members of the group then take turns reading aloud the names on the slips they have been given. In reply to each petition, the group may pray aloud "Lord, let them see the light of Faith" or some similar brief response. Meeting participants are invited to bring the slips home, place them under or near a crucifix, and pray daily for the prodigals whose names are written on them.

What Does a Meeting Look Like?

It is very important to stress the need to preserve confidentiality within the St. Monica Ministry group. In submitting their intentions, members of the parish community are trusting the St. Monica Ministry community to simply pray for their prodigals, not to gossip, speculate, or lay blame. It is a holy privilege for us to lift up those prodigals in prayer.

<u>Closing Prayer</u>

St. Augustine's poetic "Breathe in me" prayer to the Holy Spirit – included in the sample meeting agenda on page 35 - is a fitting close to a meeting. Written by St. Monica's own prodigal son-turned-saint, it expresses a yearning for sanctification. Our recitation of the prayer is a plea to the Holy Spirit to infuse us with His gifts, knowing that it is by our example that our prodigals might come to know Christ, and to ultimately embrace the Faith that He founded. The "Breathe in me" prayer is short enough that it may be included on the meeting agenda sheet.

The St. Monica Ministry™ Holy Hour of Petition and Hope

Each month, the St. Monica Ministry™ holds a Holy Hour of Petition and Hope. The Holy Hour is a powerful and moving devotion, in which we gather to worship Our Lord in the Most Blessed Sacrament, to ask for His Mercy, and to invoke St. Monica's intercession for the return of our prodigals to the Faith.

At the St. Monica Ministry™ Holy Hours held at the ministry's home parish, a different priest or deacon presides each time; however, the format of the Holy Hour does not vary from month to month.

There are several elements that distinguish a St. Monica Ministry™ Holy Hour from the standard Holy Hour. Although the inclusion or omission of these elements has no bearing whatsoever on the efficacy of our prayers, or on the number of graces that Our Lord chooses to bestow, they are nonetheless important. The signing of the Book of Petition and Hope, the lighting of Candles of Entreaty, and the praying of the Rosary of Supplication for Our Prodigals all help to strengthen our sense of community, nurture our hope, and renew our sense of purpose.

Basic Supplies

At the rear of the church should be a small but prominently placed table, holding items for participants to pick up as they enter. These items are:

1. Holy Hour programs;

2. Rosaries (contained in a basket or other small receptacle);

3. Optional are a framed image of the ministry's official icon of St. Monica, "Prayer of the St. Monica Ministry™ to its Patron" prayer cards, and trifolds containing the "Rosary of Supplication for Our Prodigals" meditations. A chapter may request any of these materials by emailing StMonicaMinistry27@gmail.com. If requesting trifolds, please bear in mind that they are costly to produce, so a donation would be especially appreciated. Alternatively, copies of the "Rosary of Supplication" meditations (see page 23), may be printed for participants' use.

Candles of Entreaty

In the center aisle, towards the front of the church, should be a table on which are placed the Candles of Entreaty. Trial and error (and a few burnt fingers) have proven that, for our purposes, it is best to use candles in plastic holders, since these are lightweight and do not conduct heat as do glass holders. What we use at our home parish are

Inserta-Lites, which are available online from several church goods suppliers. Candles should be lighted shortly before the start of the Holy Hour, so that participants need only pick up the lighted candles and carry them to the altar during the designated period.

A second table should be placed at the foot of the altar. Participants will place the lighted Candles of Entreaty – which represent their prayers for their prodigals - on this table during the musical meditation. Once participants have put down their lighted candles, it isn't unusual for them to linger before the altar, pouring out their hearts to Our Lord in the Most Blessed Sacrament. To accommodate those who want to spend a minute or two in prayer, a kneeler may be placed in front of the altar.

<u>The Book of Petition and Hope</u>

When she was close to death, St. Monica expressed indifference regarding the place of her burial, pointing out that "Nothing is far from God." Indeed, God is always with us. Even in their darkest moments, our prodigals are never so far removed from God that their salvation is out of reach.

The Book of Petition and Hope is a tangible sign of this truth, as through it we express both our dependence upon God and our hope in His Mercy. The Book of Petition and Hope – a.k.a. "St. Monica's Lost & Found" - contains pages on which may be written the names of prodigals, as well as petitions for the prodigals' return to the Faith.

The Book of Petition and Hope – along with a few pens - should be on a table, lectern, or podium near to the table on which participants will place their Candles of Entreaty. During the musical meditation, participants are invited to write the names of their prodigals in the Book of Petition and Hope, along with a prayer for the prodigals' return. At each Holy Hour, the book with its names will be present as a symbol of our prayers.

Icon of St. Monica

The St. Monica Ministry's™ official icon of St. Monica was written by Fr. K., a retired priest of the Diocese of Allentown, who has asked to remain anonymous. In gratitude for the time and effort that Fr. K. expended in the writing of the icon, please say a prayer for Father's intentions.

A framed copy of the St. Monica Ministry's™ official icon of St. Monica should be displayed during the monthly Holy Hour of Petition and Hope. Since Our Eucharistic Lord is always the focus of a Holy Hour, the icon should be placed in such a way that, while it may be seen and venerated, it will in no way obscure or draw attention away from the Most Blessed Sacrament.

Note that it is customary for an icon to be blessed by a priest prior to the use of the icon as an object of veneration. In the home parish of the St. Monica Ministry™, the blessing of the St. Monica icon was given at the end of a Holy Hour, immediately after Reposition of the Blessed Sacrament, by the priest who wrote the icon. If it can be arranged, it would be especially meaningful to have your group's icon blessed by a priest who has some connection with the chapter, perhaps as an advisor or as a spiritual director for its members.

The St. Monica Ministry "Rosary of Supplication for Our Prodigals": Meditations for Each of the Twenty Mysteries of the Rosary

Since the thirteenth century, the rosary as we know it has been a powerful tool for conversion. Trusting in its power to change hearts, the members of the St. Monica Ministry pray the Rosary of Supplication for Our Prodigals. This special rosary includes original meditations that speak to both the needs of prodigals and to the yearning of those who are praying for their loved ones' return. Each meditation either parallels or contrasts the stated mystery with something in our own, or in our prodigals', lives. A decade of the Rosary of Supplication for Our Prodigals is recited at each Holy Hour of Petition and Hope.

The Glorious Mysteries

<u>The Resurrection of Our Lord</u>

It was not until she heard Him speak her name that Mary Magdalene recognized the Risen Lord. Mary, our mother, please pray that our prodigals should hear Our Lord's voice and come to recognize Jesus as their own Beloved Master.

The Ascension of Our Lord

Before He ascended into heaven, Jesus said, "Behold, I am with you always, until the end of the age." Mary, our mother, help us to remember that, no matter how far our prodigals wander, they will always be under God's loving gaze.

The Descent of the Holy Spirit

On the day of Pentecost, the Holy Spirit filled the apostles with the knowledge of truth so that they might bear witness to the Gospel. Mary, our mother, pray that our prodigals should embrace the truths of our Holy Faith with renewed zeal.

The Assumption of the Blessed Virgin into Heaven

The Assumption of Our Lady into heaven has been likened to the arising of incense to God. Mary, our mother, we ask that you take and transform our prayers of petition, and make them as pleasing to God as incense before His throne.

The Coronation of Our Lady

At her Coronation, Mary became Queen of Heaven and earth. Mary, our mother, you who are pleased to give gifts to your children, we ask that you give the gift of faith to our prodigals, that they may come to serve you as their Queen, and your Son as their only King.

The Joyful Mysteries

<u>The Annunciation</u>

Despite her initial apprehension at the words of the angel Gabriel, Mary gave God her "fiat," confident that His Will would be accomplished in her. Mary, our mother, help us to trust that God's Will will ultimately be fulfilled in our prodigals.

<u>The Visitation</u>

In the reunion of Mary and Elizabeth, and the meeting of the unborn Jesus and John the Baptist, we see an embodiment of the communion of saints. Mary, our mother, pray that our prodigals should soon rejoin the faithful as members of Christ's mystical Body.

<u>The Nativity of Our Lord</u>

Mary, our mother, within the low and earthy confines of a stable, you showed the newborn Jesus to all who sought Him. Help us always, even in the least favorable circumstances, to show the face of Christ to our prodigals.

<u>The Presentation in the Temple</u>

Mary, our mother, at Jesus' presentation, Simeon prophesied that your motherhood would be a source of both suffering and joy. Although our prodigals' separation from the Church causes us suffering, we hope by your intercession to one day experience the joy of our prodigals' return.

The Finding in the Temple

Mary, our mother, when after three harrowing days you found Jesus in His Father's house, your joy knew no bounds. Pray that our prodigals' search for truth should lead them to their Heavenly Father's house, and to the Truth by which they will be sanctified.

The Luminous Mysteries

<u>The Baptism of Jesus</u>

In allowing Himself to be baptized by John, Jesus set an example of profound humility. Mary, our mother, we ask that you obtain humility for our prodigals, so that they will willingly submit to the teachings of the Church.

<u>The Wedding Feast at Cana</u>

Mary, our mother, when the wine ran out at the wedding feast, you trusted that Jesus would make things right. Following your example, we turn to your Son in confident expectation, knowing that He alone can change the water of our prodigals' disbelief into the wine of faith.

<u>The Proclamation of the Kingdom of God</u>

At the beginning of His public ministry, Jesus exhorted the people to "Repent, and believe in the Gospel." Mary, our mother, we implore you to help our prodigals to recognize their errors and to seek forgiveness.

<u>The Transfiguration</u>

St. Luke tells us that, when St. Peter beheld the transfigured Jesus, he was so taken aback that He did not know what he was saying. Mary, our mother, please ask your spouse, the Holy Spirit, to give us words that will help transform the hearts of our prodigals.

The Institution of the Eucharist

Mary, our mother, you are called Our Lady of the Blessed Sacrament because Jesus first took flesh through your consent. Please obtain for our prodigals the grace to recognize Our Lord's Body and Blood in the Most Holy Eucharist.

The Sorrowful Mysteries

The Agony in the Garden

Although we cannot fully understand the mystery of Jesus' suffering at Gethsemane, we can identify with Our Lord's anguish at the reality of sin. Mary, our mother, help us not to despair at our prodigals' sins, but instead to entrust our loved ones to God's mercy.

The Scourging at the Pillar

Mary, our mother, it was with a mother's empathy that you suffered the excruciating pains of your Son's scourging. As we grieve our prodigals' want of consoling faith, help us to offer up our sufferings for the sake of their return.

The Crowning with Thorns

Mary, our mother, in the minds of our prodigals, truth has been smothered by error. Obtain for our prodigals the gift of discernment, that their darkened intellects should be pierced by the light of truth.

The Carrying of the Cross

Mary, our mother, many of our prodigals are carrying the heavy guilt of past sins. Pray that our prodigals should come to know the liberating truth of God's unfailing forgiveness.

The Crucifixion

Although the effort caused Him unimaginable suffering, Jesus spoke the words, "Behold your mother" from the cross. Mary, our mother, help our prodigals to realize that, in this dark and confusing world, you are ever their life, their sweetness, and their hope.

The "Wayfaring St. Monica" Program

When her son Augustine set sail for Rome, St. Monica hiked up her tunic and boarded a boat in pursuit, even though ocean travel in those days was nothing like the cruise line experience of today. And when Augustine left Rome for Milan, St. Monica followed, despite the challenges of the journey. After Augustine was baptized in Milan, he and his mother set sail for their home in Algeria, though St. Monica would fall ill and die in Ostia, a Roman seaport.

Although she acted out of necessity rather than out of a desire to see the world,

St. Monica did her share of traveling. This is evidenced by the pilgrim's staff with which she is often pictured. St. Monica's unflagging pursuit of her wayward son is the inspiration for the St. Monica Ministry's "Wayfaring St. Monica" program.

All that is needed to implement the program is a chapter's framed image of the icon, a few families or individuals who are willing to "host" the icon in their homes, and an individual to serve as coordinator. The coordinator is responsible for scheduling visits of the icon to the hosts' homes, and providing copies of the Wayfaring St. Monica Devotional, which contains a recommended program for Wayfaring St. Monica visits. (The devotional, a reproducible PDF, is available upon request.) At the close of each month's Holy Hour, the coordinator will give the icon to the family or individual that is slated to host it for the upcoming week. During the week-long hosting period, the icon will be displayed in the home, in a place where it may be seen and venerated. Invitations to "visit with St. Monica" may be extended to family, friends, neighbors, and fellow parishioners. So as to reap the benefits of communal prayer, a specific day and time should be designated for the visit. If possible, transportation should be provided to those who, on account of age or infirmity, may not be able to attend unassisted.

At the close of the program as outlined in the Wayfaring St. Monica Devotional, it is recommended that refreshments be offered, since they contribute to a relaxed atmosphere that is conducive to conversation and sharing.

The "Wayfaring St. Monica" program offers

(1) an option for community prayer for those who would like to attend St. Monica Ministry Holy Hours or meetings, but are unable to do so;

(2) a chance to spread devotion to St. Monica beyond the parish community;

(3) an opportunity to spend time in private prayer before the official icon of the St. Monica

Ministry's patron saint.

The program offers some flexibility regarding the length of the hosting period. While it would be practical for the icon to be picked up after a Holy Hour and returned just prior to the following Holy Hour, a host might, over the intervening four weeks, grow so accustomed to having the icon in his home that he ceases to notice it. For this reason, a hosting period of one week is recommended; however, it is up to the coordinator of a chapter's "Wayfaring St. Monica" program to determine a suitable hosting period, based on factors such as the number of hosting volunteers and the accessibility of hosts' homes.

A St. Monica Ministry™ chapter may also choose to include its Book of Petition and Hope in its "Wayfaring St. Monica" program. Since those whom a host invites to "visit with St. Monica" may be non-parishioners who would not normally attend a St. Monica Ministry Holy Hour at the chapter's home church, inviting them to write the names of their prodigals in the Book of Petition and Hope would be a lovely gesture of spiritual solidarity. During the hosting period, the book would be displayed near the St. Monica icon as a reminder to pray, not only for our own prodigals, but also for the fallen-away who are outside of our own family and friend circles. If a chapter decided to make the Book of Petition and Hope part of its program, the book would wayfare from home to home along with St. Monica.

Prayer of the St. Monica Ministry to its Patron

Good St. Monica,
please implore God's mercy on our prodigal sons and daughters,
that they may come to know, accept, and cherish
the unconditional love of their Heavenly Father.

Good St. Monica,
obtain for me a measure of your virtues,
that my fallen-away loved ones
should come to know Christ through my example.

Good St. Monica,
intercede for those of my family and friends
who are walking in darkness,
that they should return to the ineffable light of our holy Faith.

Good St. Monica,
pray that I should seek and accept
God's will in all things
through Jesus Christ, our Lord. Amen.

St. Monica Ministry Sample Meeting Agenda

7:00pm-7:05pm – Recitation, Prayer of the St. Monica Ministry

7:10pm-7:20 - Welcome / Introductions

7:20pm-7:35pm - Shares

7:35pm-7:50pm – Reading aloud of submitted intentions; Recitation of Rosary

7:50pm-8:20pm - Book discussion: Chapter xx, pp. xx

8:20pm-8:25pm – Closing prayer

"Lord, as we go forth this evening, we ask that You send Your Spirit to accompany us. We pray in the words of St. Augustine:

Breathe in me, O Holy Spirit, that my thoughts may all be holy. Act in me, O Holy Spirit, that my work, too, may be holy. Draw my heart, O Holy Spirit, that I love but what is holy. Strengthen me, O Holy Spirit, to defend all that is holy. Guard me, then, O Holy Spirit, that I always may be holy. Amen."

8:25pm - Farewells / optional fellowship

Recommended Reading

Please note that, while each of the books listed is worth reading and reflecting upon, not all will lend themselves to in-meeting discussion. It is up to each individual St. Monica Ministry chapter to select the book for discussion that is best suited to the tastes and preferences of the chapter's members.

Aquilina, Mike, and Mark W Sullivan. *St. Monica and the Power of Persistent Prayer*. Our Sunday Visitor, 26 Apr. 2013.

Armstrong, Patti Maguire. *What Would Monica Do?* Ascension Press, 22 Aug. 2022.

Bougaud, Emile. *The Life of Saint Monica.* Forgotten Books, 1900.

Calloway, Donald H. *No Turning Back*. Marian Press - Association of Marian Helpers, 15 Jan. 2010.

Forbes, F A. *Saint Monica: Model of Christian Mothers.* TAN Books, 1 May 1998.

Green, Maggie. *The Saint Monica Club*. Sophia Institute Press, 24 Oct. 2019.

Kirby, Jeffrey. *Way of the Cross for Loved Ones Who Have Left the Faith*. Our Sunday Visitor, 18 Sept. 2020.

Noble, Theresa. *The Prodigal You Love: Inviting Loved Ones Back To Church*. Pauline Books & Media, 2019.

Vogt, Brandon. *Return: How to Draw Your Child back to Church*. Winter Spring, Fl, Numinous Books, 2015.

www.ingramcontent.com/pod-product-compliance
Lightning Source LLC
Chambersburg PA
CBHW070750050426
42449CB00010B/2400